# My First Pocket Guide

# LOUISIANA

I0808331

By Carole Marsh

Correlates with Louisiana's SSCS Social Studies Content Standards

THE LOUISIANA EXPERIENCE

# The GALLOPADE GANG

Carole Marsh
Bob Longmeyer
Chad Beard
Cecil Anderson
Steven Saint-Laurent
Karin Petersen
Billie Walburn
Doug Boston
Jill Sanders
William Nesbitt, Jr.
Kathy Zimmer
Wanda Coats
Terry Briggs
Jackie Clayton
Pam Dufresne
Cranston Davenport
Lisa Stanley
Antoinette Miller
Victoria DeJoy
Tena Simpson

Published by GALLOPADE INTERNATIONAL

www.louisianaexperience.com
800-536-2GET • www.gallopade.com


Character Illustrations by Lucyna A. M. Green.


***Gallopade is proud to be a member of these educational organizations and associations:***

NSSEA

ASCD

SHOPA MEMBER
School, Home, & Office Products Association

## Other Louisiana Experience Products

- The Louisiana Experience!
- The BIG Louisiana Reproducible Activity Book
- The Louisiana Coloring Book
- My First Book About Louisiana!
- Louisiana "Jography": A Fun Run Through Our State
- Louisiana Jeopardy!: Answers and Questions About Our State
- The Louisiana Experience! Sticker Pack
- The Louisiana Experience! Poster/Map
- Discover Louisiana CD-ROM
- Louisiana "Geo" Bingo Game
- Louisiana "Histo" Bingo Game

## A Word From the Author... (okay, a few words)...

Hi!

Here's your own handy pocket guide about the great state of Louisiana! It really will fit in a pocket–I tested it. And it really will be useful when you want to know a fact you forgot, to bone up for a test, or when your teacher says, "I wonder . . ." and you have the answer–instantly! Wow, I'm impressed!

Get smart, have fun!

Carole Marsh

Louisiana Basics explores your state's symbols and their special meanings!

Louisiana Geography digs up the what's where in your state!

Louisiana History is like traveling through time to some of your state's great moments!

Louisiana People introduces you to famous personalities and your next-door neighbors!

Louisiana Places shows you where you might enjoy your next family vacation!

Louisiana Nature—no preservatives here, just what Mother Nature gave to Louisiana!

All the real fun stuff that we just HAD to save for its own section!

# Who Named You?

Louisiana's official state name is...

State Name

# Louisiana

OFFICIAL: appointed, authorized, or approved by a government or organization

## Statehood: April 30, 1812

Louisiana was the 18th state to ratify the Constitution.

# A Name of Royal Proportions!



French explorer René-Robert Cavelier, Sieur de La Salle, named the area Louisiana in honor of King Louis XIV. La Salle claimed the region for France in 1682. La Salle originally planned to become a priest. After his superiors told him he needed to study more before they would send him on a mission trip to China, he left the priesthood to become an explorer and treasure-seeker.

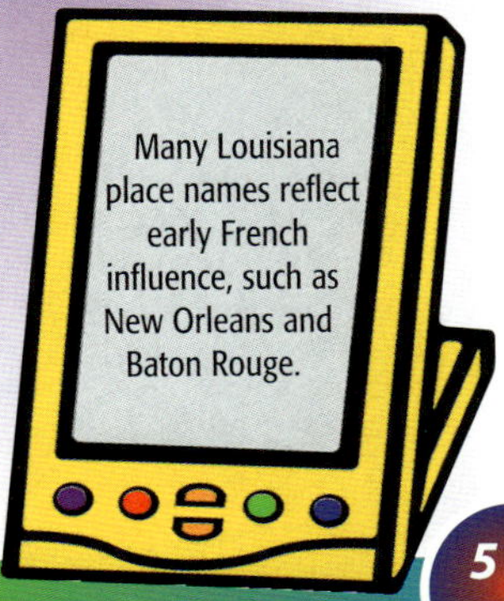

# Who Are You Calling Names?

State Nicknames

Louisiana is not the only name by which our state is recognized. Like many other states, Louisiana has an official nickname.

## The Pelican State

*Pelicans are common in gulf areas, and the bird is greatly admired by Louisianians.*

# State Capital: Baton Rouge

## Since 1849

In 1722, the village of Nouvelle Orléans (New Orleans) was named the capital of Louisiana by Jean-Baptiste Le Moyne, Sieur de Bienville. New Orleans became the center of political and economic power. Some Louisianians pressured government officials to move the capital to another city. In 1849, Baton Rouge was named the capital.

As Civil War battles moved closer to Louisiana, Baton Rouge was threatened. The capital was relocated to Opelousas in 1863, but only stayed there for a few months. The government moved the capital to Shreveport as the Union Army quickly approached.

In 1882, Baton Rouge became the capital once more, and this time it stayed there! It is a good place for the capital due to its central location and port facilities.

The state capitol was built in 1932 while Louisiana's famous governor, Huey P. Long, was in office. At 34 stories tall, it is the tallest public building in the country. Steps leading up to the capitol have the names of the states inscribed on them.

Word Definition

CAPITAL: a town or city that is the official seat of government

CAPITOL: the building in which the government officials meet

# Who's in Charge Here?

Louisiana's GOVERNMENT has three branches:

- **LEGISLATIVE**
  - *The legislative branch is called the General Assembly.*
  - Two houses: the Senate (39 members), and the House of Representatives (105 members)
- **EXECUTIVE**
  - Governor, lieutenant governor, secretary of state, attorney general, state treasurer, and other commissioners
- **JUDICIAL**
  - Supreme Court has six associate judges. Lesser courts include the Courts of Appeal and District Courts.

Louisiana's judges use the Code Napoléon to issue rulings. This means rather than relying on previous court decisions or customs of the citizens, they use a strict set of rules—or code of law—to decide cases.

# State Flag

Spanish and French flags flew over Louisiana before the state legislature finally settled on its current state flag in 1912. The flag features a nesting mother pelican feeding her three babies. The state's motto, "Union, Justice & Confidence," is in a banner beneath the nest.

# State Seal & Motto

## State Seal

The state seal was adopted on April 30, 1902, and like the flag, features the nesting mother pelican and her babies. Other versions of the seal also included a pelican, sometimes with as many as 12 chicks!

## State Motto

*Louisiana's state motto is...* **Union, Justice, and Confidence**

Louisiana's first territorial governor, William C. C. Claiborne, admired the pelican so much that he included it on all his official correspondence.

Word Definition

MOTTO: a sentence, phrase, or word expressing the spirit or purpose of an organization or group

# Eastern Brown Pelican

Brown Pelicans are large gray-brown birds that generally live near bodies of water, including oceans, bays, inlets, and beaches. Pelicans mainly feed on fish, which they catch by scooping up water in their large bills, and pouches. Mother Pelicans are so devoted to their young that they will feed them pieces of their own flesh when they can't find any other food. Most Pelicans have broods of only three chicks at a time.

A 4-week-old Pelican eats about 5 pounds (2.3 kilograms) of fish a day!

# Bald Cypress

State Tree

Louisiana's swampy areas are the right environment for moss-draped Bald Cypress trees to grow. The Cypress is prized for being a good building material. Its wood is durable and doesn't rot as quickly as other woods. Short cone-shaped extensions grow from the Cypress' roots, which are usually underwater in the swampy areas. These are called knees.

## State Wildflower:

# *Louisiana Iris*

The Louisiana Iris adds a splash of color to the Louisiana swamps. The flowers bloom in shades from pale blue to the deepest purple. They thrive in the damp, swampy marshland.



## State Flower:

# *Magnolia*

The magnolia, with white blossoms and a balmy fragrance, is a member of the ever-green family.

## State Crustacean:
## Crawfish

Crawfish look like small lobsters. Usually Crawfish are less than 6 inches (15 centimeters) long. They're also a popular food in Louisiana and a main ingredient in many recipes. The Crawfish supply in Louisiana has decreased to the point that the state started a licensing program. Fishermen have to obtain a license from the state in order to catch Crawfish. Louisiana is the Crawfish capital of the world!

## State Mammal:
## Black Bear

Black Bears spend a lot of their time trying to stay out of sight. They do not like to have contact with humans. They also spend a lot of time searching for food. Black Bears eat berries, acorns, and honey.

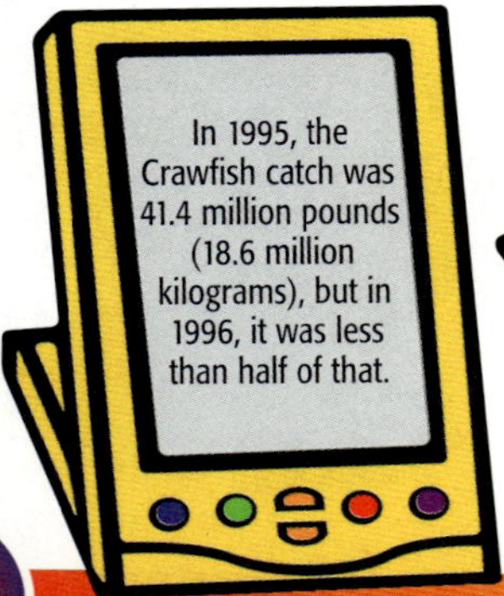

# State Reptile:
# Alligator

Louisiana's freshwater wetlands make it the perfect home for Alligators, the state reptile. Alligators can grow to lengths of 16 feet (4.8 meters). When an Alligator is hunting, sometimes all you can see are its eyes and nose above the water.

# State Amphibian:
# Green Tree Frog

Another swamp dweller that has state recognition in Louisiana is the Green Tree Frog. This frog is known by other names as well, including the Fried Bacon Frog, the Cowbell Frog, and the Bell Frog.

**RIDDLE:** What does the Louisiana state reptile call the state amphibian?

ANSWER: A SNACK

# State Dog



## Catahoula Leopard Dog

The Louisiana state dog has adapted well to its environment. The Catahoula Leopard Dog is actually a cross between the Indians' hunting dogs, Catahouls (Catahoul means "dogs of the clear water"), and the War Dogs that came with the Spanish in the 1500s. Webs have formed between the Catahoula Leopard Dogs' toes because they need to be able to track game through swampy land. The dog's coat is rough, and spotted, of course. They also have interesting eyes which are milky white, green, or yellow-brown.

# Diatonic Accordion

The Diatonic Accordion is the Louisiana state musical instrument. It provides one of the most identifiable sounds for the music that is common to the area. This Accordion is also known as the Cajun Accordion. While the Accordion is used often in Cajun songs, it has German roots. Immigrants who came to Louisiana in the mid-1870s from Germany first introduced the instrument.

State Musical Instrument

## State Gemstone:

# Agate

Agate can be found throughout Louisiana. It is a member of the quartz family. Agates can appear striped or banded and contain several colors.



## State Fossil:

# Petrified Palmwood

Wood becomes like stone—or petrified—after hot, silica-filled waters cover it for long periods of time. In some cases, this is so complete that even the cell structure is preserved. In Louisiana, Palmwood petrified, becoming hard as a rock.

## State Colors:

# Gold, White, Blue

# Honeybee

## – Apis mellifera

Honey is a major agricultural product from Louisiana. It has been collected in Louisiana since the early 1800s. Honeybees contribute to Louisiana's economy by producing honey and cross-pollinating more than 50 state crops. To produce one pound of honey, more than 550 honeybees have to visit at least 2.5 million flowers! In early Louisiana, honey was widely used as a sweetener. Today, you can buy home-grown honey at many roadside stands.

Honeybees carry pollen from flower to flower—helping them reproduce. Bees do special dances to show each other where the flowers are.

# White Perch



The state fish is also known by two other names—the Sac-au-lait and the White Crappie. The fish often grow to be 1 foot (30.5 centimeters) long, weigh about 2 pounds (1 kilogram), and make good fried fish!

Here's a recipe you can use for Perch.

## Louisiana Pan-fried Perch

Combine a beaten egg with 2 tablespoons of water. Take 4 cleaned perch and dip them in the egg mixture. Mix 3/4 cup crushed saltine crackers or cornmeal with 1/2 teaspoon salt and a dash of black pepper. Roll egged fish in meal. Fry fish in hot oil for 4-5 minutes on each side until browned. Drain on paper towels.

# State Map

## The State of Louisiana

The outline of the state of Louisiana is shaped a little like the shoe that the little old woman lived in with all her children!

# State Location



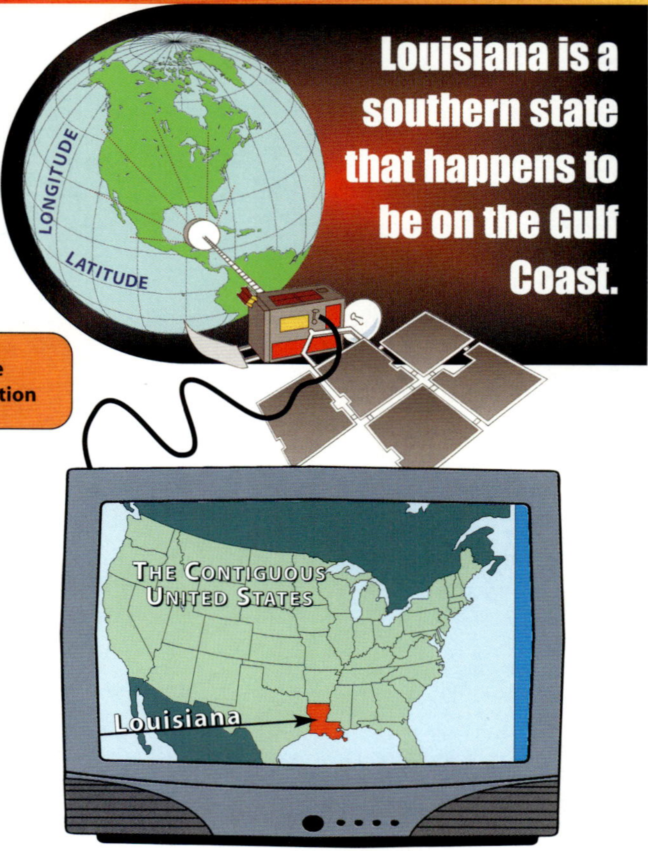


**Word Definition**

LATITUDE: Imaginary lines which run horizontally east and west around the globe
LONGITUDE: Imaginary lines which run vertically north and south around the globe

# On The Border!

## These border Louisiana:

**States:**

Texas Arkansas Mississippi

**Bodies of water:**

Mississippi River Gulf of Mexico
Sabine River Pearl River



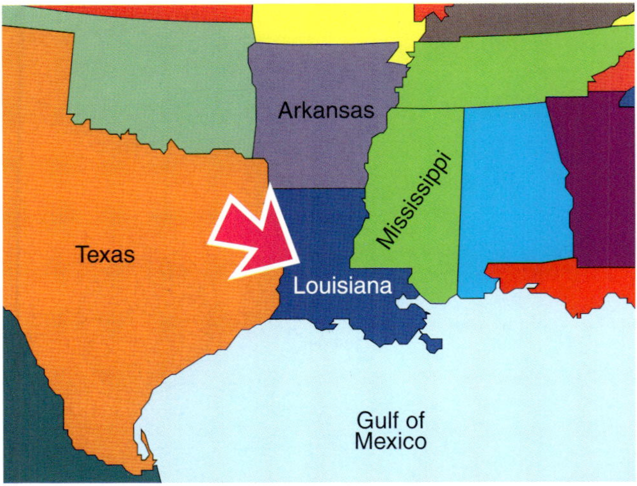

# I'll Take the Low Road...



Louisiana is about 236 miles (380 kilometers) from east to west...or west to east. Either way, it's a long drive!

**Total Area: Approx. 49,650 square miles (128,584 square kilometers)**

**Land Area: Approx. 43,566 square miles (112,827 square kilometers)**

Louisiana is 237 miles (381 kilometers) from north to south...or south to north. Either way, it's still a long drive!

# You Take the High Road!

**HIGHEST POINT**

Driskill Mountain—535 feet (163 meters)

Driskill Mountain was named for James Christopher "Grancer" Driskill, who moved from Georgia and settled near the mountain in the 1830s. Many of his descendants still live in the area. Millions of years ago, Driskill Mountain was much higher, but erosion has worn the rocks down. Driskill Mountain is part of Nacogodches Wold, which is a high plain without any trees.



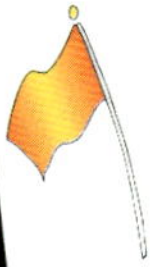

**LOWEST POINT**

5 feet (1.5 meters) below sea level—near New Orleans

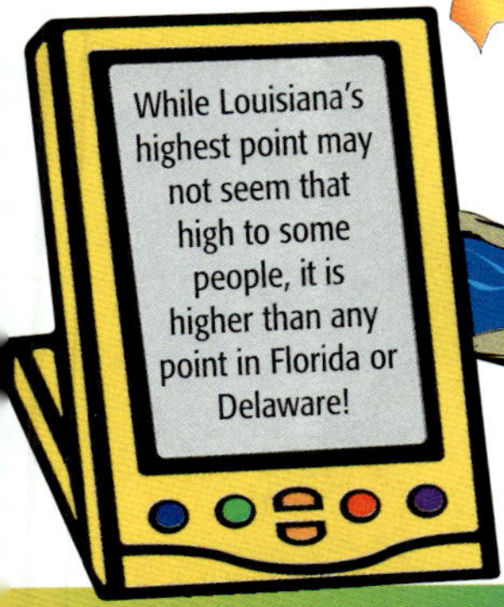

# Parish the Thought!

Louisiana is divided into 64 parishes.

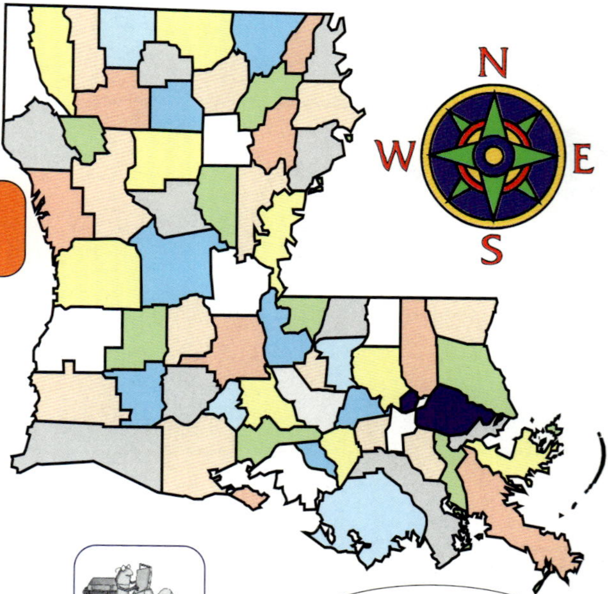


State Parishes

Word Definition

PARISH: an administrative subdivision of a state or territory

Sulfur

Sand

Gravel

Petroleum

**Forests cover 21,000 square miles (54,000 square kilometers) of Louisiana.**

*Deep-water Ports:*

- **New Orleans**
- **South Louisiana**
- **Baton Rouge**
- **Port of Lake Charles**
- **Port of St. Bernard**

The Port of South Louisiana leads all national ports in tonnage. Almost 185 million tons (168 million metric tons) of cargo go through it each year!

# Weather, Or Not?!

Because it's near the coast, Louisiana has a semitropical climate in the southern part of the state, and is moderate in the north. The weather is muggy in the summer and cool in the winter.



Highest temperature: 114°F (46°C) at Plain Dealing on August 10, 1936

°F=Degrees Fahrenheit °C=Degrees Celsius

Lowest temperature: -16°F (-27°C) at Minden on February 13, 1899

A deadly tornado hit Mississippi in May 1840. Two weeks later, a boat that had been docked at Natchez was found near Baton Rouge with 51 corpses on board!

# Back On Top

Louisiana lies entirely within the Gulf Coastal Plain. Some of the landforms found in this state are bayous, deltas, swamps, alluvial plains, chênières (islands in the marsh), marshland, rivers, lakes, and even a small mountain.

Word Definition

TOPOGRAPHY: the detailed mapping of the features of a small area or district

# King of the Hill

## DOMES

Once upon a time, long, long ago, the land of Louisiana was submerged under a shallow sea. As the sea evaporated, it left behind lots of salt. As the land changed, the salt rose above the heavier sand and mud and made high domes. There are 204 of these domes in Louisiana. One of the highest is Weeks Island. It is 160 feet (48 meters) taller than the marshland around it.



## HILLS

One of the most hilly regions is the Kisatchie Hills in western Louisiana. The Tunica Hills are in the eastern part of the state.

# Major Rivers

## A River Runs Through It!

Because of the possibility of flooding, the people of Louisiana have made walls called "levees" along the rivers to help control the raging waters. These levees run about 1,650 miles (2,655 kilometers) along the river banks!



In the 1800s, steamboats were "the way to go" on the Mississippi River. In 1812, the *New Orleans* was the first to paddle into *(where else?)* New Orleans. By 1840, 400 boats were sailing up and down the river, carrying passengers and freight. You can still take a ride today on one of several steamboats sailing the Mighty Mississippi River.

**RIVERS**
- Mississippi
- Red
- Ouachita
- Sabine
- Pearl
- Calcasieu
- Black

**BAYOUS**
- Teche
- Lafourche
- Dugdemona
- Dorcheat
- D'Arbonne

# Gone Fishin'

- White Lake
- Lake Borgne
- Caddo Lake
- Lake Bisteneau
- Toledo Bend Reservoir
- Lake Pontchartrain
- Calcasieu Lake

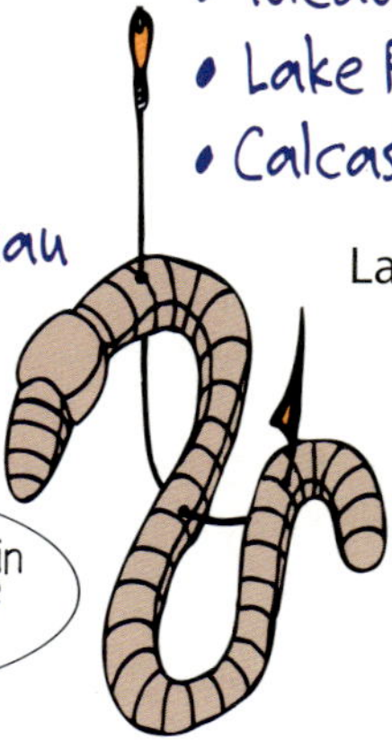

Lake Pontchartrain is the largest lake in Louisiana, measuring 625 square miles (1,619 square kilometers) in area. It is called a brackish lake, which means its water is part saltwater.

# Cities & Towns

## ARE YOU A CITY MOUSE... OR COUNTRY MOUSE?

Have you heard of these wonderful Louisiana town, city, or crossroad names? Perhaps you can start your own list!



LARGER TOWNS:

- New Orleans
- Baton Rouge
- Shreveport
- Lafayette
- Kenner
- Lake Charles
- Monroe
- Bossier City
- Alexandria

SMALLER TOWNS:

- Bunkie
- Cut Off
- Dry Prong
- Many
- Noble
- Pioneer
- Plain Dealing
- Sulphur
- Sun
- Waterproof

# Transportation

## Major Interstate Highways

I-49, I-10, I-12, I-20, I-55
There are 55,000 miles (88,495 kilometers) of roads and highways in Louisiana.

The longest bridge in the world, the Lake Pontchartrain Causeway, is in Louisiana. It is 24 miles (38.6 kilometers) long.



## Railroads

More than 4,000 miles (6,436 kilometers) of railroad track chug across Louisiana.

## Major Airports

International airports are at New Orleans and Alexandria.

## Ports

New Orleans, Baton Rouge, Lake Charles, Port of South Louisiana, Shreveport, Plaquemine, St. Bernard, Alexandria, Louisiana Offshore Oil Port (LOOP)

# Timeline

| | |
|---|---|
| 1541 | Hernando De Soto becomes the first European to see the Mississippi River |
| 1682 | Territory of Louisiana is claimed for France by René-Robert Cavelier, Sieur de La Salle |
| 1763 | Under the Treaty of Paris, Louisiana belongs to Spain |
| 1764 | Acadian immigrants arrive from Canada |
| 1800 | Spain cedes Louisiana to France in the treaty of San Ildefonso |
| 1803 | United States buys Louisiana from France |
| 1812 | Louisiana is admitted to the U.S. as the 18th state |
| 1815 | British are defeated at Battle of New Orleans |
| 1861 | Louisiana secedes from the Union and joins the Confederacy |
| 1868 | Louisiana is readmitted to the Union |
| 1896 | U.S. Supreme Court rules in favor of Louisiana's "separate but equal" law permitting racial segregation in public facilities |
| 1901 | Oil is discovered near Jennings |
| 1935 | Senator Huey Long is assassinated at the state capitol |
| 1964 | Civil rights laws are enacted by U.S. Congress |
| 1977 | Ernest N. "Dutch" Morial is elected first African-American mayor of New Orleans |
| 1984 | Louisiana's World Exposition is held in New Orleans |
| 2001 | On to the 21st century! |

# Here come the humans!

Early History

Thousands of years ago, ancient peoples inhabited Louisiana. They may have originally come across a frozen bridge of land between Asia and Alaska. If so, they slowly traveled east until some settled in what would one day become the state of Louisiana.

The early Louisiana culture is even older than South America's Mayas and Incas. Artifacts found on Avery Island date back to 700 BC.

# Native Americans Once Ruled!

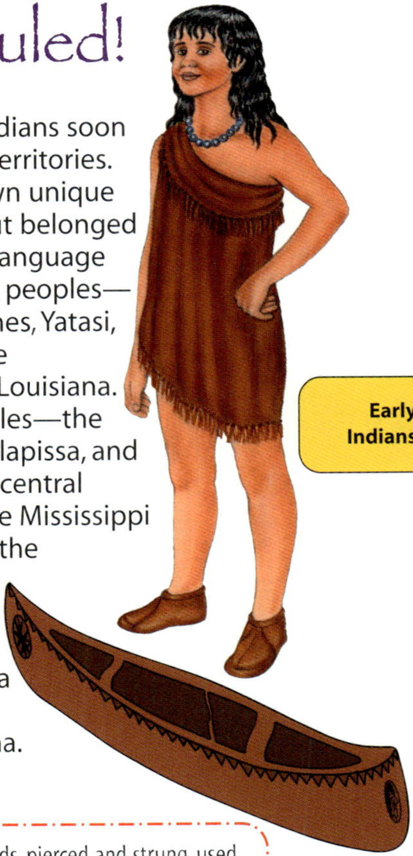

Louisiana's early Indians soon organized into tribal territories. Each group had its own unique customs and dress, but belonged to one of three main language groups. The Caddoan peoples—the Caddo, Natchitoches, Yatasi, and Adai—lived in the northwestern part of Louisiana. The Muskogean peoples—the Houma, Choctaw, Acolapissa, and Taensa—lived in east central Louisiana and near the Mississippi River. The Tunicans—the Chitimacha, Atakapa, and smaller groups—lived along the Gulf Coast. The small Koroa group lived in northeastern Louisiana.

Word Definition

WAMPUM: beads, pierced and strung, used by Indians as money, or for ornaments or ceremonies.

# Land Ho!

Hernando De Soto was the first European to explore Louisiana in 1541 and 1542. He sailed from Cuba to the American coast leading soldiers, slaves, and missionaries into northern Louisiana and Arkansas in search of Christian converts and GOLD! Unfortunately, De Soto and his men brought diseases with them that devastated the Native Americans. De Soto died of a fever on May 21, 1542.



In 1682, the Mississippi Valley was claimed for France by René-Robert Cavelier, Sieur de La Salle, who named it in honor of King Louis XIV.

# Home, Sweet Home

Pierre Le Moyne, Sieur d'Iberville founded the royal French colony of Louisiana in 1699. The first permanent European settlement was established in 1714 at Natchitoches on the Red River.

When King Louis XIV died, his 5 year-old great-grandson took the throne as Louis XV. Since Louis XV was just a kid, his uncle, Philippe II, Duc d'Orléans, was named regent (ruler). Scottish financier John Law received permission to colonize Louisiana in 1717 from Philippe II. Law sold worthless stock to wealthy Europeans to raise money for the colony, a venture that was called the Mississippi Bubble.

Settlers arrived from Europe and Canada to make the new colony of Louisiana their home, sweet home!

# Key Crops

Rice, cotton, and sugarcane were important crops for the Europeans who came to Louisiana. A few large plantations were established, but most of the crops were grown by small farmers.

Rice was first grown in Louisiana in the early 18th century. It was grown along the Mississippi River and along the southwest Gulf Coast. Rice was exported to Europe by 1750.



Emanuel Prudhomme first grew cotton on his plantation near Natchitoches in 1718. The invention of the cotton gin in 1793, a machine that separates cotton from the seeds and hull, helped expand the market for cotton.

A new way to granulate sugar on a large scale was developed in 1795. Refineries were built in central locations.

Much labor was needed to cultivate the crops on the large plantations. Between 1720 and 1731, nearly 3,000 slaves from Africa were brought to Louisiana.

# Sunken Treasure

After the War of 1812, pirate Jean Lafitte reportedly moved his operation away from New Orleans, but it remained his biggest market. He would slip into New Orleans through Barataria Bay. One night, the Coast Guard nearly caught one of Lafitte's sloops loaded with treasure. The pirates scuttled the ship on Sabine Lake. People still hunt for the buried treasure today!

# Room to Grow!

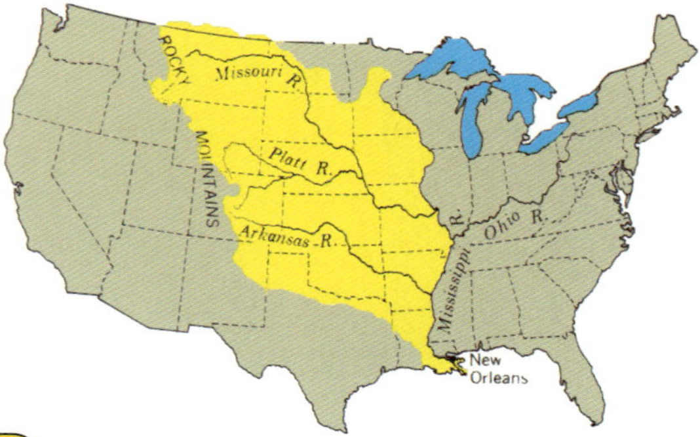


**Louisiana Purchase**

American President Thomas Jefferson wanted the Mississippi River system and New Orleans to be part of the United States. He sent statesmen to Paris to buy the land from the French emperor, Napoléon Bonaparte. Napoléon didn't want to sell, but he needed money to finance his wars in Europe.

In 1803, Napoléon sold the Louisiana territory to the United States for $15 million. In other words, the U.S. bought 300,000,000 acres (120,000,000 hectares) of land for 5¢ an acre (.4 hectare).

The Louisiana Purchase included the present states of Louisiana, Arkansas, Iowa, North Dakota, South Dakota, Nebraska, and parts of Kansas, Colorado, Wyoming, Montana, and Minnesota. What a deal!

# Of Human Bondage

As a Southern state, Louisiana was dependent on the plantation system of agriculture. Thousands of the slaves brought to America from Africa worked on these large farms, growing and harvesting crops.

At one time, a third of Louisiana's population were black men, women, and children—all slaves—who could be sold, and the families divided at any time their owners chose to do so.

Slaves worked hard, as they were forced to do, and life was hard on the plantation. Long days, hard labor, disease, and bad weather made plantation life one of misery.

Many slaves shared unique talents, such as creating some of the favorite foods we enjoy today from recipes or seeds they brought from Africa. Slave women created quilts with secret designs which could help slaves trying to escape find their way along the Underground Railroad.

Most Louisianians never owned slaves. Usually only the wealthy or large plantation owners owned slaves.

Word Definition

ABOLITIONIST: person who believed slavery was wrong and should be abolished.

# Brother

The Civil War was fought over slavery and states' rights. Southern states, with plantations and slaves, were on one side of this battle. Northern states, who opposed slavery or had no need for it, were on the other side. Some states remained neutral on the issue.



Louisiana seceded from the Union and joined the newly formed Confederate States of America in 1861. Fifty-six thousand Louisianians joined the Confederate Army, while 10,000 more joined home guard units. Louisianians also joined the Union Army—5,224 whites and 24,052 blacks.

Word Definition

RECONSTRUCTION: the recovery and rebuilding period following the Civil War.

# The Civil War

## vs. Brother

The Civil War was also called the War Between the States. Soldiers often found themselves fighting against former friends and neighbors, even brother against brother. Those who did survive often went home without an arm, leg, or both, since amputation was the "cure" for most battlefield wounds. More Americans were killed during the Civil War than during World Wars I and II together!



In 1863, the Emancipation Proclamation, issued by U.S. president Abraham Lincoln, freed the slaves still under Confederate control. Some slaves became sharecroppers; others went to Northern states to work in factories.

# Get It In Writing!

Declaration of Independence, 1776

U.S. Constitution written, 1787

First state constitution, 1812

State constitution of 1868 gave African-Americans the right to vote

Present state constitution and new Bill of Rights went into effect, 1975

# Immigrants

## WELCOME TO AMERICA!

Louisianians have come to Louisiana from other states and many other countries on almost every continent! As time goes by, Louisiana's population has grown more diverse. This means that people of different races and from different cultures and ethnic backgrounds have moved to Louisiana.

Louisiana's Creoles are the descendents of early French and Spanish settlers and African slaves. Cajuns are the descendants of French Canadians (Acadians), who were forced to leave Canada after the British took control. German immigrants came in 1721 and settled north of New Orleans in an area known as *La Côte des Allemands* (the German Coast). Thousands of Hispanics and Asians from many countries have also made Louisiana their home. Irish laborers worked on the New Basin Canal, the link between Lake Pontchartrain and the Mississippi River.

African-Americans came to Louisiana as slaves from West Africa, but freemen from Santo Domingo and other Carribean islands have left their imprint on Louisiana.

# Disasters & Catastrophes!

## 1853

Outbreak of yellow fever in New Orleans; more than 11,000 people die

## 1893

Hurricane, Chenitre Caminada; 1,800 people are killed



## 1908

Longest and deadliest twister of all time travels 158 miles from Weiss, Louisiana to Winchester, Mississippi, causes 143 deaths

## 1927

Record winter rainfall causes the Mississippi River to overflow; worst flood in state history leaves 300,000 homeless

## 1957

Hurricane Audrey; 400-500 people die

# Legal Stuff

## 1724

Jean Baptiste Le Moyne, Sieur de Bienville, governor of the French colony, issues the Black Code aimed at controlling slave behavior and revolts and activities of free blacks.

## 1896

U.S. Supreme Court rules in favor of Louisiana's "separate but equal" law permitting racial segregation in public facilities, most notably in public schools.

## 1898

State Constitution is revised to allow "grandfather clause" permitting some illiterate whites to bypass literacy requirement for voting, but disqualifies African-American voters.

## 1958

New Orleans puts an end to segregation on city buses.

## 1964

Civil rights law passes that forbids discrimination in most public schools.

# Women and Children

As early as **1727**, Catholic nuns in New Orleans teach white, Native American, and African-American girls to read and write.

Louisiana requires all children between the ages of 6 and 16 to attend school in **1916**.



Congress approves women's suffrage (the right to vote) in **1920**.

Lucille May Grace, registrar of the State Land Office, campaigns for governor in **1952**. She loses in the primaries, but opens the way for other women to run for state office.

U.S. Supreme Court rules women to be routinely called for jury duty in **1975**. Until then, Louisiana women had to make a request in writing for the chance to serve on a jury.

# Fight!, Fight!, Fight!

Wars that Louisianians participated in:

- **War of 1812**
- **Mexican-American War**
- **Civil War**
- **Spanish-American War**
- **World War I**
- **World War II**
- **Korean War**
- **Vietnam War**
- **Persian Gulf War**

# "Laissez les bon temps rouller!"

## *—Let the good times roll—*

Mardi Gras (Fat Tuesday) is the French term for Shrove Tuesday. Shrove Tuesday is the day before the start of Lent, the 40-day period of prayer and penitence before Easter. The best known Mardi Gras carnival in the U.S. is held in New Orleans. All festivities end at midnight on Mardi Gras day.

Mardi Gras is the end of a two-month period of parties and celebrations given by krewes, organizations with a secret membership, which exist to take part in Mardi Gras. Each krewe has a king and a court and may hold a parade. The parades start two weeks before Mardi Gras and feature elaborate floats. During parades, costumed paraders throw plastic beads and trinkets to the crowds.

King cakes iced in purple, green, and gold are enjoyed during Mardi Gras. The cakes honor Rex, the king of Mardi Gras, and a little doll is baked inside each cake. Whoever finds the doll is "king" of the party and has to either bring the next cake or host another King Cake party. The colors stand for royalty, purple; wealth, gold; and faith, green.



The country-style Mardi Gras held in Louisiana is called the Courir du Mardi Gras. Costumed riders go from farm to farm collecting the ingredients for a giant gumbo served at a community feast. Cajun bands traveling on flatbed trucks usually go with the rider.

Mardi Gras costumes are displayed year-round at the Louisiana State Museum located in the old U.S. Mint in New Orleans.

# Indian Tribes

- Caddo
- Natchitoches
- Yatasi
- Adai
- Houma
- Choctaw
- Acolapissa
- Taensa
- Tunica
- Chitimacha
- Atakapa
- Koroa
- Muskhogeans

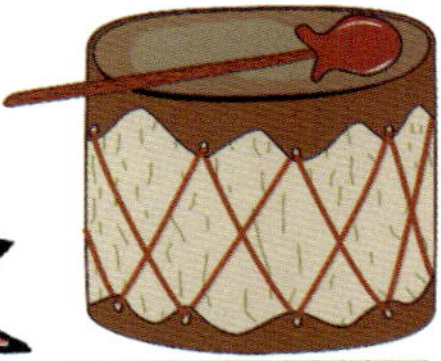

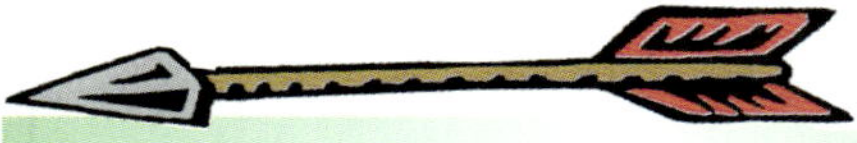

Indians of Louisiana could not have known that the coming of the white man would mean an end to the way of life they had known for hundreds of years!

The Chitimachas have lived in Louisiana for centuries. The word *chitimacha* means "men altogether red." Acadians, French-speaking refugees from Canada, settled in Louisiana. The two cultures merged when Acadians and the Chitimachas married. The Chitimacha Indian Reservation is located in Charenton and has a museum, trading post, and a school. The tribe hosts a Green Corn Festival around the Fourth of July every summer.

The bird-shaped mound at Poverty Point is believed to be around 3,000 years old. It is more than 70 feet (21 meters) high.

# Here, There, Everywhere!

*In **1519**, Alonso Alvarez de Pineda explored the Gulf of Mexico and discovered the mouth of the Mississippi River.*

*In **1541**, Hernando De Soto, a Spaniard, was the first European to explore Louisiana. He and 600 soldiers, or conquistadors, were looking for cities of gold—instead they found the Mississippi River!*



*In **1682**, French explorer René-Robert Cavelier, Sieur de La Salle, claimed the Mississippi Valley for France and named it in honor of Louis XIV.*

*The French colony of Louisiana was founded by another French explorer, Pierre Le Moyne, Sieur d'Iberville, in **1699**.*

# Founding Fathers

JOHN LAW was a financier from Scotland who got the permission of Philippe II of France to colonize Louisiana.

JEAN-BAPTISTE LE MOYNE, Sieur de Bienville, founded New Orleans in 1718 and named it in honor of Philippe II, Duc d'Orléans.

JOSEPH BROSSARD was the leader of the Acadians—French Canadians from Nova Scotia evicted from their homes in 1755.

Italian HENRI (ENRICO) DE TONTI was with La Salle on his exploration of Louisiana. De Tonti became an important European contact with the Native Americans and laid groundwork to establish the new colony.

LOUIS JUCHEREAU DE ST. DENIS founded the first permanent settlement in the Mississippi Valley. It was Fort St. Jean Baptiste (Natchitoches).

# Founding Mothers

MOTHER CABRINI was a Catholic nun born in Lombardy, Italy. She built day care centers and schools in New Orleans and was the first U.S. citizen to be canonized.

In 1727, the URSULINE NUNS established a convent in New Orleans and founded hospitals and schools.

In 1952, **KERMIT A. PARKER**, a pharmacist from New Orleans, became the first African-American to run for governor of Louisiana.

Louisiana was the first state to commission an African-American as a military officer. **MAJOR JOSEPH SAVARY** was commissioned during the War of 1812.

**ALEXANDER PIERRE "A.P." TUREAUD** was an attorney. In the 1930s and 1940s, he won legal battles that helped overturn the state's segregation policies. He was a leader and role model for young African-Americans!



**ERNEST N. "DUTCH" MORIAL** was a law partner of A.P. Tureaud. He was the first African-American elected to the Louisiana state legislature since the Civil War! Morial later became mayor of New Orleans for two terms!

**JORDAN NOBLE** was a young African-American drummer who rallied American troops in the Battle of New Orleans.

## DID SOMEONE SAY BOO!?

Have you heard the scary ghost story about the Beauregard-Keyes house? The French Quarter mansion built in the 1820s once belonged to Confederate General Pierre Gustave Toutant Beauregard. Today, the restored mansion is a popular inn where guests are greeted and entertained by guides in costumes. At night, a ghostly reenactment of the famous Civil War battle at Shiloh occurs. General Beauregard rides his great white horse through the ballroom's huge double doors. The battle rages through the night becoming more terrifying and bloody—then, as the morning light breaks, the battle scene disappears!

DO YOU BELIEVE IN GHOSTS?

The longest boxing match took place in New Orleans on April 6, 1893 between Andy Brown and Jack Burke. It went 110 rounds, lasted for more than seven hours, and ended in a draw!

The Superdome in New Orleans is a 27-story arena that seats more than 95,000 spectators. It's the world's largest enclosed stadium! You can see the National Football League's Saints come marching in to win!

## SPORTS FIGURES:

Kordell Stewart–football player

Nat "Sweetwater" Clifton–Harlem Globetrotter basketball player

Freddie Spencer–motorcycle racer

Kay McDaniel–tennis player



Leigh Ann Lloyd Legg–weight lifter, set an American record in 1988 for total pounds lifted

## Olympic Athletes:

Ben Sheets–baseball

John Lovell–sailing

Ashley Tappin–swimming

LaMark Carter–track and field

# Entertainers

- ★ *Kitty Carlisle–singer, actress*
- ★ *Van Cliburn–concert pianist*
- ★ *Fats Domino–musician*
- ★ *Louis Moreau Gottschalk–pianist, composer*
- ★ *Al Hirt–trumpeter*
- ★ *Mahalia Jackson–gospel singer*

- ★ *Dorothy Lamour–actress*
- ★ *Jerry Lee Lewis–singer*
- ★ *Huddie "Leadbelly" Ledbetter–composer and folk singer*
- ★ *Ray Walston–actor*

- ★ *Aaron Neville–musician*
- ★ *Pete Fountain–Dixieland jazz clarinetist*
- ★ *Sidney Becht–jazz musician*

**????????** What was the famous movie about the French Quarter starring Marlon Brando, Vivien Leigh, Kim Hunter, and Karl Malden?

**ANSWER:** *A Streetcar Named Desire* based on the Pulitzer Prize-winning play by Tennessee Williams

# Authors & Artists

Lillian Hellman-playwright

Lucien Marcon-New Orleans sculptor

Cokie Roberts-journalist

John James Audubon-naturalist and artist, famous for illustrations and paintings of North American birds, painted the wild turkey at Beech Woods

Arna Wendell Bontemps-author and poet

A. de Batz-artist who painted Native Americans

Truman Capote-author

Roark Bradford-author

George Rodrigue-Cajun artist



Clementine Hunter-first a field hand and cook, became a famous painter known for her bright colors and expressive portraits

Grace Elizabeth King-historian and author

Lyle Saxon-historian and author

Anne Rice-author (Dracula's a big fan!)

Do you know what one of John James Audubon's other professions was?

**ANSWER:** dancing instructor

# All That Jazz

A special type of music called jazz was born in America in the 1900s that blends African rhythms and Italian brass-band percussion. Its roots come from the sacred spirituals and work songs of African slaves. The style that came to be known as jazz was mostly instrumental at first and grew up in the city of New Orleans.

Cornetist Charles "Buddy" Bolden was one of the founders of New Orleans jazz. Many other great jazz musicians followed including Scott Joplin, Ferdinand "Jelly Roll" Morton, Louis "Satchmo" Armstrong, Louis Prima, the Marsalis family, Duke Ellington, and Ornette Coleman.

A jazz tradition continues at funerals in New Orleans even today! The music is sad and slow at the cemetery. Then, the funeral procession parades home led by a band playing joyous, hand-clapping, parasol-twirling music in celebration of the person's life!

You can hear jazz at festivals and events throughout Louisiana and even played by musicians on the streets of New Orleans!

# Very Important People

MICHAEL DE BAKEY–surgeon

GEOFFREY BEENE–fashion designer

GENERAL ANDREW JACKSON–fought in Louisiana during the War of 1812; led American troops to victory against the Creek Nation

BRYANT GUMBEL–broadcast journalist

PAUL PRUDHOMME–chef, restaurateur, and author

JIM BOWIE–frontiersman

ALFRED MOUTON–Confederate general

EDMUND MCILHENNY–invented Tabasco sauce in 1868 (some like it really, really hot!)

BERNARD E. RANDOLPH–Air Force general

# More VIPs

HARRY LEE–Chinese-American, elected sheriff of Jefferson Parish, served several terms; known as the Chinese Cowboy because he always wore a cowboy hat and boots

PIRATE JEAN LAFITTE–fought alongside American troops, Choctaw Indians, free blacks, and slaves against the British during the War of 1812

TINA SOON–born in Shanghai; well-known Louisiana journalist

OLIVER POLLOCK–Louisiana Irishman, gave his fortune to the Spanish army who defeated the British army in the Battle of Pensacola



GEORGE WASHINGTON CABLE–historian and author, famous for Creole studies

PIERRE GUSTAV TOUTANT BEAUREGARD–Confederate general

ANGELO SOCOLA–improved techniques to grow and process rice

# Good Guys and Gals:

In 1905, DR. QUITMAN KOHNKE of New Orleans asked for an ordinance that required water supplies be screened in an effort to battle yellow fever. DR. CARLOS FINLAY, a Cuban, discovered that the disease was carried by mosquitoes. Dr. Kohnke's solution keeps mosquitoes from breeding, and yellow fever is no longer a problem.

DOLORES SPIKE was chancellor of Southern University in Baton Rouge from 1988 to 1991. She was the first African-American woman in the nation to head a major liberal arts college.



# Bad Guy:

General Benjamin Butler was a Union general during the Civil War. He issued an order directed to the ladies of New Orleans stating "any woman insulting a member of the federal forces in any way would be severely punished." The ladies nicknamed him "Beast" Butler!

# Political Leaders

**HUEY P. LONG**–popular governor nicknamed "The Kingfish" led a "Share-the-Wealth" program for Louisiana

**LUCILLE MAY GRACE**–first woman to run for governor of Louisiana

**WILLIAM CHARLES COLE (C.C.) CLAIBORNE**–first territorial governor

**MARY LANDRIEU**–Louisiana's first woman senator, fought for social causes and women's issues

**LINDY BOGGS**–first female U.S. representative

**DAVID C. TREEN**–elected in 1979, first Republican governor since 1877



**LEANDER PEREZ**–powerful political "boss" of Plaquemine Parish for decades

**MARTIN BEHRMAN**–first German mayor of New Orleans

**EDWARD DOUGLASS WHITE**–U.S. Supreme Court justice

**EDWIN EDWARDS**–three term governor, increased state spending for education and tourism

# Keeping the Faith

SAINT LOUIS CATHEDRAL, NEW ORLEANS–triple-steepled cathedral completed in 1794

OUR LADY OF VICTORY CATHOLIC CHURCH, NEW ORLEANS–built in 1845; part of the Ursuline Convent

SAINT MARY'S ASSUMPTION CHURCH, NEW ORLEANS–completed in 1860; has a 142-foot (43-m) tower that changes from a square to an octagonal shape at the roof level

TOURO SYNAGOGUE, NEW ORLEANS–built in 1907

SAINT JOHN'S EPISCOPAL CHURCH, THIBODAUX–consecrated in 1845; the oldest Episcopal church in the state

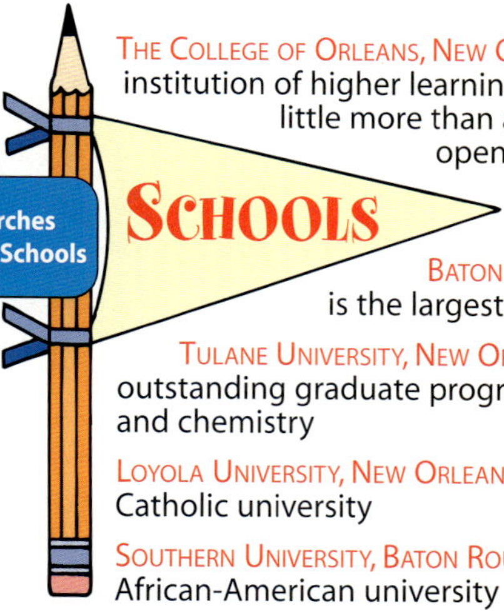


THE COLLEGE OF ORLEANS, NEW ORLEANS–first institution of higher learning in Louisiana, lasted little more than a decade after opening in 1811

LOUISIANA STATE UNIVERSITY, BATON ROUGE–this university is the largest in the state

TULANE UNIVERSITY, NEW ORLEANS–noted for outstanding graduate programs in law, medicine, and chemistry

LOYOLA UNIVERSITY, NEW ORLEANS–private Roman Catholic university

SOUTHERN UNIVERSITY, BATON ROUGE–largest African-American university in the state

# HISTORIC SITES

**Fort Miro Historic Site**, Monroe–an outpost built by the Spanish

**Poverty Point State Commemorative Area**, Monroe–one of the most significant archaeological sites in North America

**Harrisonburg Indian Mound**–sacred ground of Natchez or Ouachita tribes

**Pargoud Mound**, Monroe–ceremonial mounds left by the Ouachita Indians

**Acadian Village**, Lafayette–re-creation of 19th century Acadian town

In St. Martinville stands a very special tree—the Evangeline Oak. In the graveyard of St. Martin de Tours Church is a statue of a girl named Evangeline. Both commemorate the arrival of the Acadians and Henry Wadsworth Longfellow's poem about a young girl separated from her love during their trip from Nova Scotia.



# PARKS

**Jean Lafitte National Historic Park and Preserve**, New Orleans

**Cane River Creole National Historic Park**

**New Orleans Jazz National Historic Park**

**Vicksburg National Military Park**–a portion of this Mississippi park is in Louisiana

# Early Residency

***1850 House***, New Orleans–built for Baroness de Pontalba

***Hermann-Grima House***, New Orleans–built in 1831

***Haunted House***, New Orleans–built in 1832; supposed to have ghosts of mistreated slaves killed in a house fire

***Strachan House***, New Orleans–where Jefferson Davis died on a visit in December 1889

***Turn of the Century House***, Morgan City

***Shadows-on-the-Teche***, New Iberia

***Arlington House***, Washington–three-story brick house; one of the largest plantation houses in bayou country

***Homeplace***, Washington–a raised Creole cottage built in 1826



***Evergreen***, on the River Road–one of the few Louisiana plantations with intact buildings

***San Francisco***, on the River Road–built in 1854; modeled after a steamboat

***Nottoway***, on the River Road–built in 1859; called the White Castle

***Edwin Epps House***, Bunkie–built in 1852; commemorates the life of the slave Solomon Northup

***Little Eva Plantation***, Cloutierville–may have been the inspiration for Harriet Beecher Stowe's setting of *Uncle Tom's Cabin*

## A few of Louisiana's famous Forts

- **Fort Saint Jean Baptiste**, Natchitoches–French fort built in 1714 on the north bank of the Red River
- **Fort Beauregard**, Harrisonburg–built by Confederates in 1862; seized and destroyed later; a park commemorates the site
- **Fort Polk**, near Leesville–established in 1941

## A few of Louisiana's famous Battlefields

- **Mansfield Battle Park**–Forty-acre (16 hectare) site commemorating two Civil War battles fought nearby
- **Chalmette Plantation Battle Site**, New Orleans–final battle of the War of 1812 occurred here on January 8, 1815; the war had officially ended on December 24, but news had not reached the British troops in the United States; battle that made General Andrew Jackson famous

# Libraries

Check out the following special state libraries! (Do you have a library card? Have you worn it out yet?!)

**Louisiana State Library,** Baton Rouge–provides information and books to the entire state

**Tulane University Library,** New Orleans

**Loyola University Library,** New Orleans

**Northwestern State University Library,** Natchitoches–collections of Louisiana folklore and Native American history

**Libraries at Grambling State University, Southern University, and Xavier University** house special collections in African-American studies

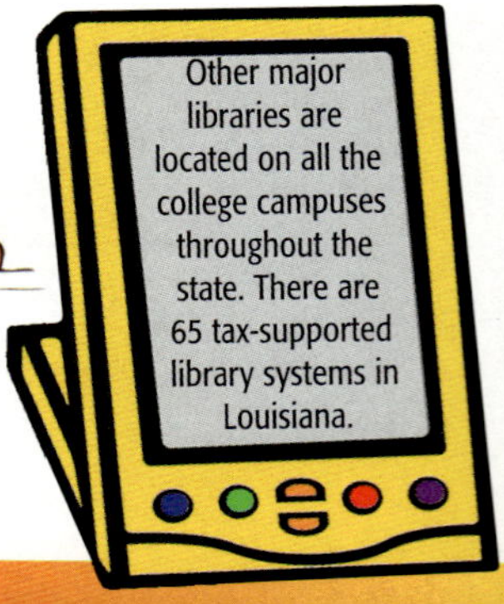

# Places to Go

**Greater Baton Rouge Zoo**

**Magnolia Mound Plantation,** Baton Rouge

**Audubon Park & Zoological Garden,** New Orleans

**Louisiana Children's Museum,** New Orleans

**Louisiana Nature & Science Center,** New Orleans

**Walter B. Jacobs Memorial Nature Park,** Shreveport

**Louisiana Arboretum,** Ville Platte

**Pioneer Heritage Center,** Shreveport

**New Orleans Pharmacy Museum**

**Melrose Plantation Home Complex,** Melrose

**D'Arbonne National Wildlife Refuge,** Farmerville

**Rosedown Plantation,** Francisville

**French Quarter *(Vieux Carré)*,** New Orleans

# Museums

**Louisiana State University Rural Life Museum,**
Burden Plantation, near Baton Rouge
**Museum of Natural Science,** Baton Rouge
**The Rice Museum,** Crowley
**Fort Polk Military Museum**
**Lafayette Natural History Museum and Planetarium**
**Confederate Museum,** New Orleans
**Louisiana State Museum,** New Orleans
**Pitot House Museum,** New Orleans
**Louisiana Tech Museum,** Ruston
**Firefighters' Museum,** Baton Rouge
**Emy-Lou Bidenharn Bible Research Museum,**
Monroe
**Brimestone Museum,** Sulphur
**American Italian Heritage Museum,** New Orleans

# Lest We Forget

## MONUMENTS

Huey P. Long Monument,
Baton Rouge

Jackson Square,
New Orleans

## MEMORIALS

Louisiana Naval War Memorial,
Baton Rouge



R.S. Barnwell Memorial Garden and Art Center,
Shreveport

Alfred Mouton Memorial,
Lafayette

# The Arts

- Blue Dog is a famous series by Cajun artist George Rodrigue.
- A Streetcar Named Desire by Tennessee Williams is one of the most famous plays about life in the South. It is set in the steamy French Quarter of New Orleans.
- Crowley Art Association and Gallery is located in the town of Crowley. It features guided tours, festivals, workshops, and interactive exhibits.
- New Orleans Museum of Art contains paintings, sculptures, photography, and many more works of art from around the world.
- Preservation Hall in New Orleans is a mecca of traditional jazz. The greatest names in music perform there.



Word Definition

MECCA: a place that attracts people with common interests.

# Louisiana Coast

## SOME OF LOUISIANA'S ISLANDS INCLUDE:

*Avery Island*–a landlocked salt dome 7 miles (11 kilometers) south of New Iberia; Tabasco, the hot fiery sauce, is made on this island

*Pecan Island*–supposedly the old stomping ground of pirate Jean Lafitte and his men; tales of a hidden treasure on the island are plentiful

Louisiana has about 397 miles (639 kilometers) of coastline along the Gulf. If you include all of the inlets, islands, and bays you come up with a coastline of 7,721 miles (12,426 kilometers).

## SOME OF LOUISIANA'S LIGHTHOUSES INCLUDE:

*Barataria Bay Lighthouse*

*Chandeleur Island Lighthouse*

# Roads and Bridges

## SOME LOUISIANA SCENIC ROADS:

OLD SPANISH TRAIL, begins in Houma and ends in Breaux Bridge

CREOLE NATURE TRAIL, begins in Sulphur and ends in Lake Charles

LONGLEAF TRAIL SCENIC BYWAY, winds through the Kisatchie National Forest

THE RIVER ROAD, roads on the east and west banks of the Mississippi River

## SOME LOUISIANA BRIDGES:

SUNSHINE BRIDGE, Donaldsonville–located on the Mississippi River; connects Baton Rouge and New Orleans



HUEY P. LONG BRIDGE, crosses the Mississippi north of New Orleans

HALE BOGGS, crosses Mississippi upriver from New Orleans

PONCHARTRAIN CAUSEWAY, the longest bridge in the world crosses Lake Ponchartrain

# Swamps, Marshes, & Bayous

Most swamps, marshes, and bayous are found in the southern part of the state. A pirogue is as common a sight as an alligator in a swamp. Made from cypress wood logs, flat on the bottom, and pointed at both ends, a pirogue has been called a Cajun canoe. It is used to pole through bayous to catch fish, nutria, beaver, and crawfish.

## A Few of the Swamps, Marshes, and Bayous Found in Louisiana:

The Bayou Cocodrie Swamp, Atchafalaya Basin
The Swamp Gardens, Morgan City–where the 1917 movie *Tarzan* was filmed
Bayou Teche, located along Route 182
Marsh Trail, near Sabine National Wildlife Refuge
Kisatchie Bayou, a state designated natural and scenic stream

# Animals

## LOUISIANA'S ANIMALS INCLUDE:

Alligator
Beaver
Black Bear
Deer
Fox
Mink
Muskrat
Opossum
Rabbit
Raccoon
Squirrel
Wild Pigs

Alligators will dig their own ponds to make sure they have open water during dry seasons.

# Take A Walk On the Wild Side

Some of Louisiana's endangered wildlife include:

American Alligator

Bald Eagle

Brown Pelican

Loggerhead Sea Turtle

Louisiana Black Bear

Peregrine Falcon

Red-cockaded Woodpecker

West Indian Manatee

# Birds

Bald Eagle
Blackbird
Blue Heron
Blue Jay
Brown Pelican
Falcon
Grackle
Marsh Wren
Roseate Spoonbills
Sandpiper
Snowy Egret
Sparrow
Wood Duck
Woodpecker

## Legend

The crow and the peacock both had dull feathers a long time ago. To change them, the birds got some paint. The crow painted the peacock's feathers beautiful colors, but the peacock wanted to show off his feathers and threw a bucket of black paint on the crow.

# Don't let these Louisiana bugs bug you!

Ants
Beetle
Bumblebee
Butterfly
Cicada
Cricket
Dragonfly
Firefly
Grasshopper
Honeybee
Katydid
Ladybug
Mayfly
Mosquito
Termite
Walking Stick
Weevil
Yellow Jacket

Bumblebee

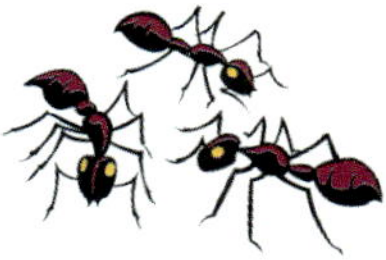
Ants

Butterfly

Ladybug

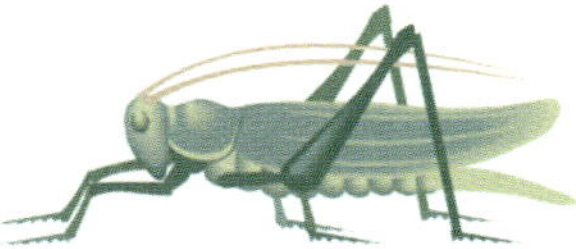
Grasshopper

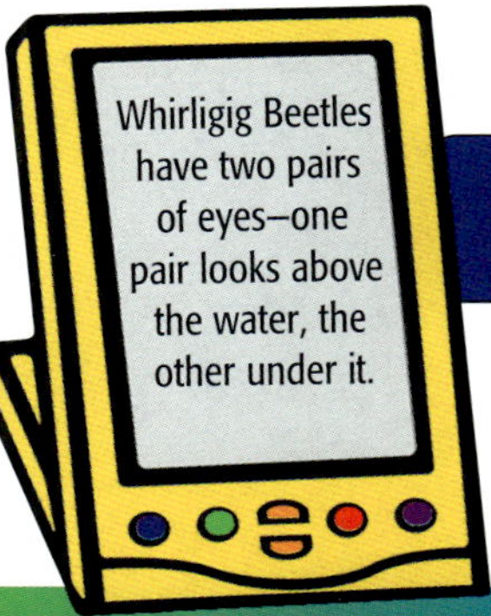

# Fish

## SWIMMING IN LOUISIANA WATERS:

- Barfish
- Bass
- Carp
- Catfish
- Crappie
- Flounder
- Mackerel
- Menhaden
- Mullet
- Paddlefish
- Red Snapper
- Sunfish
- White Perch

The weight and value of the annual catch in Louisiana is greater than that of any state except Alaska!

# Sea Critters

## In Louisiana's coastal waters, you may find:

- Crabs
- Crawfish
- Dolphins
- Eel
- Jellyfish
- Manatees
- Oysters
- Porpoises
- Sharks
- Shrimp
- Squid
- Turtles

# Seashells

She sells seashells by the Louisiana seashore!

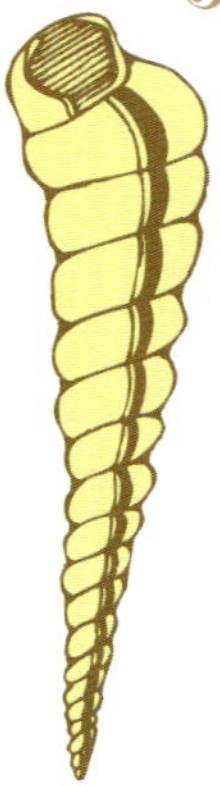

Auger Shell
Cerith
Cockle
Conch
Cone Shell
Coquina
Cowrie
Helmet Shell
Janthina
Moon Shell
Murex
Mussel
Nerite
Olive Shell
Oyster
Periwinkle
Slipper Shell
Wentletrap
Whelk
Worm Shell

Janthinas travel the ocean upside down! They are supported by a raft of foamy bubbles!

# TREEMENDOUS!

## THESE TREES GRACE THE STATE OF LOUISIANA:

**Alder**
**Bald Cypress**
**Blackgum**
**Beech**
**Elm**
**Hackberry**
**Hawthorn**
**Live Oak**
**Persimmon**
**Sourwood**
**Sycamore**

In Lafayette there's a special club for old-timers—old-time trees, that is! The Live Oak Society was founded by Dr. Edwin L. Stephens, and its members are oak trees that are 100 years old. The trees have guardians who trace their history and help preserve them. And there are club dues, too. Each tree has to "pay" 25 acorns a year which are planted and raised in nurseries to make sure there are plenty of baby oaks for the future.

Trees

# Flowers

## Are you crazy about these Louisiana wildflowers?

Aster
Blazing Star
Cattail
Chicory
Goldenrod
Ground Orchid
Lupine
Phlox
Queen Anne's Lace
Saint-Johnswort
Violet

# Cream of the Crops

## Agricultural products from Louisiana

Poultry & Eggs

Sugarcane

Alfalfa

Rice

Strawberries

Pecans

Peaches

Soybeans

Beef Cattle

Oats

Cotton

# Louisiana Potpourri

- **Spanish moss** was once used for baby diapers!
- The **Atakapa Indians** of Louisiana were said to be cannibals! Yikes!
- Some say the city of **Opelousas** is so French that the dogs don't even understand English. *Parlez-vous français? Woof!*
- Louisiana's **first oil well** spouted 7,000 gallons (26,460 liters) a day!
- **Marie Laveau** was the Queen of Voodoo.
- **Pirogues, radeaux, and barques** are all types of boats in Louisiana.
- Louisiana was the real birthplace of the **teddy bear.**
- One-third of the people in Louisiana are **Roman Catholic.**
- **New Orleans** is settling 3 inches (8 centimeters) per century.

# Festivals

**Sugar Bowl Football Game,** New Orleans–January

**World Championship Crawfish Etoufée Cook-off,**
Eunice–March

**Taste of the Bayou Food Festival,** New Orleans–March

**Holiday in Dixie,** Shreveport–April

**Louisiana Shrimp and Petroleum Festival,**
Morgan City–September

**Louisiana State Fair,**
Shreveport–October

**Natchitoches Christmas Festival of Lights,**
December

**New Orleans Jazz and Heritage Festival,** April–May

**Bridge City Gumbo Festival,** October

**Contraband Days,**
Lake Charles–May

# Holidays

# Calendar

| | | |
|---|---|---|
| Martin Luther King, Jr. Day, *3rd Monday in January* | Presidents' Day, *3rd Monday in February* | Memorial Day, *last Monday in May* |
| Independence Day, *July 4* | Columbus Day, *2nd Monday in October* | Veterans Day, *November 11* |
| Thanksgiving, *the 4th Thursday in November* | Louisiana Purchase Day, *December 20* | Christmas, *December 25* |

**Bonfires along the Mississippi River help Papa Noël, the Creole Santa Claus, find his way to New Orleans. Before the holidays, families along the river build large statues out of wood and kindling. On Christmas Eve, they set fire to the statues, which can be seen for miles along the levees.**

# Louisiana is famous for the following delicious foods!

- **Court-bouillon**–a Creole fish dish featuring wine/tomato sauce
- **Beignets and café au lait**
- **Meat pie**
- **Pralines**
- **Fried catfish**
- **Oysters Bienville**–oysters with bechamel sauce
- **Blackened redfish**
- **Smoked soft-shell crabs**
- **Boudin**–a Cajun sausage

- **Dirty rice**–pan fried leftover cooked rice sauteed with green peppers, onion, celery, stock, and giblets
- **Etoufée**–spicy Cajun stew prepared with rice and, usually, crawfish
- **Gumbo**–thick, spicy soup prepared with ingredients such as rice, sausage, chicken, and okra
- **Red beans and rice**
- **Po-boy**–a long sandwich on French bread usually stuffed with oysters, shrimp, or roast beef
- **Jambalaya**

# Louisiana Works!

The main elements of Louisiana's economy are the production of minerals—particularly oil and natural gas, but also sulphur, salt, and lignite, petroleum refining, chemical and petrochemical manufacturing, tourism, forestry, agriculture and food processing, commercial fishing, shipbuilding, and general manufacturing.

One major Louisiana import is crude oil from the Middle East. Louisiana's ports on the Gulf of Mexico are vital to the import of oil. One facility, the Louisiana Offshore Oil Port, Inc. (LOOP), is very important to this work. LOOP is located 20 miles (32 kilometers) off the coast of Lafourche Parish in the Gulf of Mexico. Large oil tankers—some as long as four football fields!—dock at LOOP and off-load their cargoes through a pipeline that goes to shore. Before LOOP, the larger tankers had to remain offshore and transfer their cargo to tankers small enough to enter the state's ports. LOOP is much more efficient and has never had a significant oil spill.

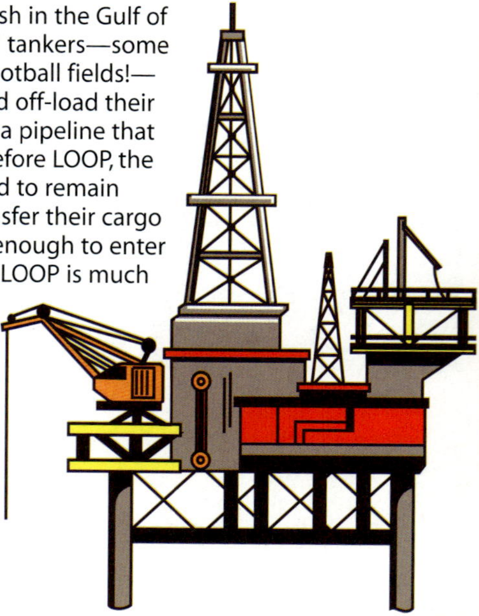

# State Books & Websites

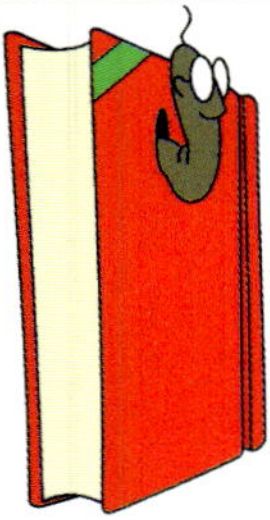

- *My First Book About Louisiana* by Carole Marsh
- *America the Beautiful: Louisiana* by Martin Hintz
- *Let's Discover the States: Louisiana* by the Aylesworths
- *The Louisiana Experience* by Carole Marsh

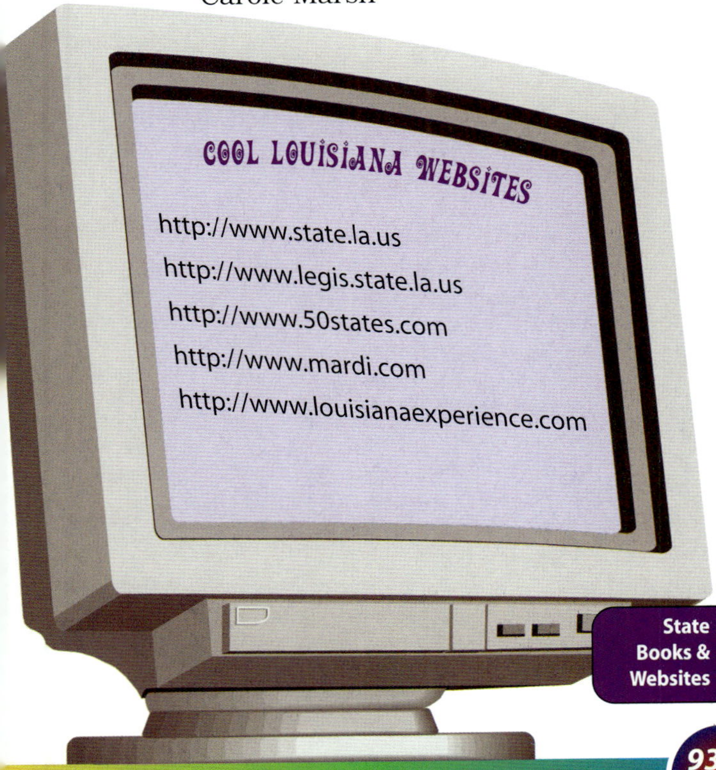

# Louisiana

## Words to Know

### Glossary Words

**Cajun**–descendants of Acadians from French Canada
**Creole**–descendants of the original French and Spanish colonists
**colony**–a region controlled by a distant country
**constitution**–a document outlining the role of a government
**emancipation**–to be set free
**fais do dos**–Cajun party with dancing and food, lasting late into the night
**gumbo**–a Creole stew
**immigrant**–a person who comes to a new country to live
**parish**–like a county; a Roman Catholic term meaning an administrative area
**revolution**–the overthrow of a government
**secede**–to voluntarily give up being part of an organized group

# Louisiana Spelling Bee

Here are some special Louisiana-related words to learn! To take the Spelling Bee, have someone call out the words and you spell them aloud or write them on a piece of paper.

| Spelling Words | | |
|---|---|---|
| | Atakapa | Louisiana |
| | Atchafalaya | Mississippi |
| | Audubon | Napoléon |
| | bayou | Natchitoches |
| | Beauregard | Opelousas |
| | Calcasieu | Ouachita |
| | Catahoula | pirogue |
| | Chitimacha | Plaquemine |
| | cuisine | Pontchartrain |
| | jambalaya | secession |
| | Kisatchie | Thibodaux |
| | Lafayette | |

# About the Author

## ABOUT THE AUTHOR...

CAROLE MARSH has been writing about Louisiana for more than 20 years. She is the author of the popular Louisiana State Stuff series for young readers and creator, along with her son, Michael Marsh, of "Louisiana Facts and Factivities," a CD-ROM widely used in Louisiana schools. The author of more than 100 Louisiana books and other supplementary educational materials on the state, Marsh is currently working on a new collection of Louisiana materials for young people. Marsh correlates her Louisiana materials to the Louisiana Social Studies Content Standards. Many of her books and other materials have been inspired by or requested by Louisiana teachers and librarians.

*The author dedicates this book to her husband, Bob Longmeyer, who has helped her with all the research ("and driving!") necessary to complete her more than 10,000 childrens' titles.*